SUMMER

AS THE EARTH TURNS

Lynn M. Stone

The Rourke Book Co., Inc.
Vero Beach, Florida 32964

Edited by Sandra A. Robinson

PHOTO CREDITS
All photos © Lynn M. Stone

Library of Congress Cataloging-in-Publication Data

Stone, Lynn M.
   Summer / by Lynn M. Stone.
      p. cm. — (As the earth turns)
   Includes index.
   ISBN 1-55916-020-9
   1. Summer—Juvenile literature. [1. Summer.] I. Title.
II. Series: Stone, Lynn M. As the earth turns.
QB837.6.S76 1994
508—dc20   93-39058
                                          CIP
                                          AC

Printed in the USA

TABLE OF CONTENTS

SUMMER

Summer is the warmest season of the year. Summer follows spring and leads to fall, or autumn.

Summer days are long and often sunny. Many young animals grow up in the summer. Plants grow quickly, producing new roots, stems, leaves and seeds. Fruits and vegetables ripen in farmers' gardens.

Many young animals, like the Columbia ground squirrel, grow up in summer

THE SUN AND THE SEASONS

The Earth spins like a round, tilting top while it travels in **orbit** around the sun. Even though it is 93 million miles away, the sun supplies the Earth's heat and light.

Each day the Earth's tilt, or angle, toward the sun changes slightly. So each day the Earth has a different amount of sunlight than the day before.

The changes in the hours of sunlight bring changes in Earth's weather and seasons.

The Earth's year-long journey around the sun brings summer and the other seasons

SUMMER NORTH AND SOUTH

During our spring and summer, the northern **hemisphere,** or half, of the Earth is tilted toward the sun. At the same time, the southern hemisphere is tilting away from the sun. The southern hemisphere has fall and winter.

During cold months in the northern hemisphere, the southern hemisphere has spring and summer.

The northern hemisphere's tilt toward the sun brings summertime, when Alaskan brown bears go fishing

SUMMER ARRIVES

Summer calls with warm, sunny days. Even summer nights, brightened by fireflies, are mild. Sometimes, though, cool air mixes with warm. That sparks great summer sky shows of thunder and lightning.

Toward the top of the Earth at the north pole, the summer sun barely sets at all. The most northern and southern parts of the world have, in their turns, the longest summer days.

Butterflies brighten the already sunny days of summer

The cold of mountain heights slows the advance of summer, which arrives late in the mountain meadows of western North America

A spider web sparkles with dew in a summer wetland

LEAVES OF SUMMER

Plants begin to grow in spring. In summer, warm days, rain and sunshine keep plants growing.

Forest trees with green leaves are a sure sign of summer. Shady branches darken the forest. Without sunlight, the forest's spring wildflowers fade away. However, sun-loving summer flowers bloom in meadows. Summer marshes fill with cattails, and grass springs up on lawns and prairies.

Late summer wildflowers and a dragonfly share a sunrise

RAISING ANIMAL BABIES

Spring is a time for nests to be built and animal babies to be born. Summer is a time for animals to begin growing up. Young animals eat well in summer. They grow quickly.

Birds born in spring can fly south in early fall. Many large animals, like deer and bears, don't grow up in just one summer.

Growing quickly in summer, this young Canada goose will be able to fly south with its parents in September

ANIMALS IN SUMMER

Summer is a busy season for animals. Birds work to find the food that will make them strong for their autumn journey south. Wolf pups learn to hunt and get along with other wolves. Three-year-old grizzly cubs learn to live without their mothers.

Butterflies and bees visit flowers. Like dazzling jewels with wings, dragonflies perch along streams.

A salad of summer greens
helps a grizzly cub to grow up

SUMMER MEANS ...

Summer means county fairs, splashing in a pool, tenting in a forest. Summer means fishing in a lake, canoeing down a wild, rushing river.

Summer means time to mow a lawn, read a book, take a hike, or watch a baseball game.

Summer means a picnic lunch, the buzz of honeybees, the crunch of corn on the cob.

Summer means a rumbling,
tumbling brook in a forest green

SUMMER AROUND THE WORLD

Summers are not the same everywhere. At the northern and southern ends of the Earth, summers are very short. At the south pole in Antarctica, the warmest days are in January. "Warm" is 40 degrees Fahrenheit!

The **equator** is an imaginary line around the middle of the Earth. The equator's angle toward the sun changes very little. The weather of countries at **sea level** near the equator is always summery.

Glossary

equator (ee KWAY ter) — the imaginary line drawn on maps around the Earth's middle at an equal distance from the north and south poles

hemisphere (HEHM iss fear) — either the northern or southern half of the Earth, using the equator as a divider

orbit (OR bit) — the path that an object follows as it repeatedly travels around another object in space

sea level (SEE LEHV uhl) — the same height, or level, as the sea

INDEX

11/00

NEW HANOVER COUNTY PUBLIC LIBRARY
201 CHESTNUT STREET
WILMINGTON, NC 28401

GAYLORD S